Keith Miller

Leadership on Demand

Mildred,

Continued success To
you and your colleagues
at AASCU!

Keith
Miller

Keith Miller

Leadership on Demand

Get Over Yourself!

LAP LAMBERT Academic Publishing

Imprint
Any brand names and product names mentioned in this book are subject to trademark, brand or patent protection and are trademarks or registered trademarks of their respective holders. The use of brand names, product names, common names, trade names, product descriptions etc. even without a particular marking in this work is in no way to be construed to mean that such names may be regarded as unrestricted in respect of trademark and brand protection legislation and could thus be used by anyone.

Cover image: www.ingimage.com

Publisher:
LAP LAMBERT Academic Publishing
is a trademark of
International Book Market Service Ltd., member of OmniScriptum Publishing Group
17 Meldrum Street, Beau Bassin 71504, Mauritius

Printed at: see last page
ISBN: 978-613-9-90631-4

LEADERSHIP ON DEMAND

Get Over Yourself!

Keith Miller, Ph.D.

Table of Contents

Underlying tenets Integrated Throughout the Book

FIVE PHASES OF TRANSLATIONAL LEADERSHIP

ZERO SUM GAIN THINKING (LEADERSHIP): The Biggest Impediment to a Competitive Advantage

THERE IS SOMETHING IN US THAT WOULD HAVE US RATHER LOOK GOOD, THAN BE GOOD.

THAT IS WHAT WE DO! THAT IS WHAT I DO! VALUES!

IF YOU DON'T SUCCEED THE FIRST TIME YOU ARE ABOUT AVERAGE.

LEADERSHIP IS THE NEW SUPPLY CHAIN

ORGANIZATIONS ARE INTERDEPENDENT

Organizations today are a microcosm of the world we live in. Our world is interdependent and so are our organizations. Partnerships are mandatory whether they are country to country, city to city, institution to institution, department to department or person to person. Virtually none of the fundamental challenges facing organizations today can be addressed in isolation. The interdependence is necessary for effectiveness and efficiency. Without partnerships or the use of relationships success is short lived and the vision of leadership is short-sighted.

People need People. Organizations need other organizations.

GOOD LEADERS START WITH THEMSELVES

Sometimes it is hard to know where to start. Good Leaders start with themselves. Good leaders on their personal and professional growth. Leaders are not handling the problems, the issues, the challenges for other people. They are doing it for themselves. You cannot be a democratic and egalitarian leader in the workplace and be an autocratic egotistical person at home. Life doesn't work that way. You are who you are. You are not the position you are in.

What you see is what you get.

Be true to thine self. In life when one door of happiness closes, another one opens. This holds true in the workplace as well. Often we look so long at the closed door that we don't see the one that has been opened for us.

Inspiration and optimism must happen inside the leader first, then, they can be spread to the masses.

"Remember the tea kettle. Though up to its neck in hot water, it continues to sing." [1]

---

[1] Gilbert, Robert. (1997). More of the Best of Bits and Pieces. The Economic Press. Fairfield, NJ. p 176.*

LEADERS SHOULD LEARN FROM THEIR EXPERIENCES, BUT MAINTAIN THEIR SPONTANEITY

Learning from experience is important. What you learn from experience is more important. Sometimes what is learned is only relevant to a particular situation. It may not apply to most situations.

Because something was learned does not mean the right thing was learned. The personal analysis is what is important. This analysis may take time.

The right choices have to be made and this will often depend on the circumstances. Longitudinal data if often difficult to get.

You know what you don't know, and you move forward anyway. This happens more than you think.

learning is
NOT
a spectator
sport.

so let's
PLAY!

Learning as a leader includes the good, the bad and the ugly.

Enjoy the ugly. Everyone has some.

FEW GREAT PEOPLE

There are few great people in the world, but many great challenges which ordinary people can address. There will not always be common goals and shared values between organizations or individuals. There always will be a level of conflict within and around the organization. Partnerships/relationships require give and take scenarios. Win/win situations are always desired, but not always possible.

Many of the better leaders are more disappointed by the things they did not do, than by the things they did do. There is a time to be flexible and there is a time to be steadfast. The challenge is to figure out which is which.

"In matters of taste, swim with the current; in matters of principle, stand like a rock.[2]

---

[2] Ibid-1, p.114.

WHERE LEADERS COME FROM

The leaders today come from poverty, tragedy, abuse etc. No obstacle was big enough to stand between them and their destiny.

When billionaire Henry Ford was asked what he would do if he lost all his fortune, he replied, "I would have it all back in five years." [3]

What would happen if you lost your job, your reputation was ruined and your supporters were wavering. Good leaders will take five years and put it all back together.

More often than not, leaders come from behind; they were the underdog!

---

[3] Ibid-1, p.176

BE VERSATILE

In regards to good leadership there are a hundred theories about how to be one. I believe there may only be one. Be versatile. Along with the versatility, leaders should have a sense of purpose, authenticity, self-awareness, intellectual honesty and the ability to navigate ambiguity, says Herman Taneja, managing editor of General Catalyst Partners, a venture capital firm.[4] "Get comfortable with being uncomfortable," says Mike Abbott of Kleiner Perkins Caufield & Byers a venture capital firm.

A key to success is to decide what you would like to do, but be willing to take some detours along the way. The detours do not have to keep you from your goals. The detours help you get the appropriate resources behind your effort. Detours include the unexpected crisis that may or may not be your fault. The crisis could be personal, it could be business, it could be both. At some point, most of us have both.

---

[4] Fortune Magazine, January 1, 2015. p.86.

"It is much easier to be critical than to be correct," said Benjamin Disraeli, former British Prime Minister. [5]

Being correct may not make you happy!

LESS MAY BE MORE

The better leaders lead without others knowing they are being led. Is less leadership better than more leadership? Some leaders subscribe to the notion that I worked hard for what I have gotten and so should they. But, no leader can promise to know all the answers, he or she can promise to listen to all the questions. They should not necessarily wish that their environment was easier to deal with, but should wish that they were better at handling it.

Since the 1980s, China began a series of reforms. It lifted an estimated 600 million people out of poverty. No nation in the history of the world has pulled as many people out of poverty in such a short period of time. [6]

What leader would have thought about China in this way? "A word to the wise is sufficient." [7]

---

[5] Ibid-1, p.46

[6] Fortune Magazine, July 25, 2011, p.52.
[7] Gilbert, Robert. (2000). Even More of the Best of Bits and Pieces. The Economic Press. Fairfield, NJ p. 80.

THE TOO LATE SYNDROME

You are always late, or you're always too late. You are always rushing or you're always playing catch up.

Timing may be everything. Some things you can control and some things you cannot control. You can control procrastination, but you cannot control Timing!

"If it is painful for you to criticize someone, you're safe in doing it; if you take pleasure in it, hold your tongue," [8]

---

[8] Ibid-1, p. 47

ORGANIZATIONS: A REFLECTION OF ITS PEOPLE

Organizations reflect the people that are in them. Often employees are clear about their ways and preferences. They are satisfied with their personal behavior. I believe that organizations that may be more loyal to their employees, decline less quickly than other organizations.

Whether you are in industry, government or education the greatest leaders are pioneers – visionaries with the courage to demand the impossible from themselves and others. They challenge people to look beyond their perceived limitations and to imagine things as they could be. They can take the impossible and not only make it possible, but make it a practical reality.

Good leaders can respond to losing as well as they can respond to winning. No one wins all the time. Good leaders have to be good winners and good losers. Good winners win gracefully and lose gracefully. Both circumstances are a team effort.

The continuum of what is possible or impossible varies from organization to organization. For the organization to stretch, individuals must stretch. They must stretch in similar ways and in the same direction. While all of this is going on, the leadership must figure out a way for both the organization and the leadership to survive.

It is not what you do for co-workers, but what you have empowered them to do for themselves that will make the organization successful.

LEADERSHIP = LISTEN + OBSTACLES + CHANGE

Leadership is about change. Most people hate change unless it is jingling in their pocket. Change is a frightening construct. Change has always been upon us and will always be upon us. It is better to create the change ourselves rather than have the change thrust upon us. It is human nature not to be happy with change, but organizations survive and excel based on their ability to change. Every environment whether it be industry, government or education is dynamic. People within organizations often survive based on their ability to change.

As the process of change unfolds the pessimists become more visible. This group is usually not the majority, but they can certainly be perceived that way. Solidify the support of one group at a time; those that are for you, those that are on the fence, then, those that are against you. However, I do understand that in some organizations there are only two groups; those that are uncertain and those that are against you. Incentives for change become essential.

Alleviate fear of the unknown. Alleviating fear of the unknown is an ongoing process. The cornerstone of the process commences with developing trust. The starting point is empathy. This is an ongoing endeavor.

Good leaders learn by doing.

Good leaders learn by watching.

Good leaders learn by listening.

"Having someone's trust is like having money in the bank. When you keep your word, it's like making a deposit into your trust fund. You have a separate trust fund for each person. Nobody's perfect. When there comes a time when you will not be able to keep your word, you will have a large enough balance of trust to draw from. Be honest." (Matt Dimaio, Motivational Speaker)[9]

Bank on building trust.

[9] Ibid-1 p. 252

GOOD LEADERSHIP TRIGGERS QUESTIONS

For leaders you can begin with a new coat of paint. Spruce up the facilities. Change the public relations activities. The challenge is to make real change that is sustainable.

Good leadership triggers questions from within and outside the organization. Some questions are:

--What is success? The notion of success may evolve over time. It will change as the environment changes.

--Can you sustain the success once you attain it?

--What will be the economic impact of the success?

--How will the success effect the core mission of the organization?

--What does the success mean for other stakeholders such as suppliers, customers, competitors, etc...

As a leader it is often better for you to ask many of these questions to the employees, because you will never know all the answers.

"Your modesty will draw attention to whatever it is you are asking about." [10]

---

[10] Ibid-1, p.100

CAN'T EVERYONE JUST GET ALONG

Because all stakeholders do not have the same perspective some people are not going to be happy with every initiative or adjustment. Too much change in an organization will disenfranchise people. Individuals within the same stakeholder group will not all agree. Controversy and leadership often equals change. Change is eminent because you can be sure that the expectation is that progress in your organization over the past decade has to be exceeded by the progress of your organization over the next decade.

Leaders are not always able to make everyone happy. Some people in and around the organization may never be happy regardless of what happens.

Challenges, pitfalls and problems are necessary for growth in being a leader. The more difficult the situation, the stronger the leader becomes. Most leaders don't know how talented they really are until adversity comes.

The better leaders are not intimidated by the difficulty of challenges, they are inspired by them.

Transform the adversity into an enjoyable challenge.

"To guard against the tendency to say 'no' too quickly, one executive keeps the following sign on his wall:

HOW TO BURY A GOOD IDEA

It will never work.

We've never done it that way before.

We're doing fine without it.

We can't afford it."

We are not ready for it."

It is not our responsibility. [11]

Much of the time it is other employees that are making these statements.

TALK IS CHEAP

At a certain level change leadership includes meandering through a labyrinth of options. Change should happen without effecting the elements that make the organization strong. Many leaders are prodigious talkers. Talk is cheap.

Doing the right thing all the time, makes for a just leader. Doing the right thing is almost always harder than doing something different. There is always a price to be paid.

Stand for something and act accordingly!

"Always do right. This will gratify some people and astonish the rest."(Mark Twain,[12]

However, there is a time and place for conservatism in leadership. It's just not as much fun as risk-taking.

---

[12] Ibid-1, p.254

INFORMING THE INFORMATION AGE

Leaders today should rethink how industries, educational institutions and governmental agencies will be relevant over the next twenty years. We will need to think about what skill-sets will constitute a competitive advantage. We even need to continue to re-think what learning modalities will be relevant in all sectors.

"See everything. Overlook a great deal. Improve a little."(Pope John XXIII)[13]

[13] Ibid-1, p.107

SOCIETY'S MOST PRESSING PROBLEM

 Society's most pressing problems are not necessarily unemployment, the education achievement gap of underserved populations, health care, international relations, or terrorism. Our most pressing problem is leadership. I am not solely referring to the leadership that exists at the top of various organizational hierarchies, I am referring to the notion of leadership throughout our organizations and society. This includes how we interact with each other and how we treat each other. It takes leadership to keep the best interests of all people in the forefront. All leaders have a responsibility to the people they directly and indirectly effect. Leaders exist at all levels in organizations and in society.

 Heroes tend to serve others, regardless of the industry.

 There is a lesson learned in everything we do.

 Heroes conquer hard times.

 "Some people think too much of themselves and too little of others."[14]

---

[14] Ibid-1, p. 56

THE JOURNEY OF A LEADER

When leadership is discussed usually what comes to mind is the organizational hierarchy. Leadership should occur horizontally, and from the bottom up as well. The journey of a good leader may not always have a clear beginning, middle or end. Good leadership is about adapting and moving forward. Take a few steps backwards, to then, take a few more steps forward. This is very difficult to do in a "what have you done for me lately" environment. There is no crystal ball. You must make sacrifices, take calculated risks and lick your wounds when you need to.

"Be like a duck. Keep calm and unruffled on the surface, but paddle like the devil underneath." [15]

---

[15] Ibid-1, p. 56

THE PERSON YOU WERE MEANT TO BE

People, generally, enjoy having a sense of mission. Everyone has a purpose. We are intended to do good works. Certainly the goals and objectives of the organization are paramount, but a major goal for individuals is to become the person you are intended to become. As individual goals are reached, those around the person reap the benefits. Every once in a while you get a glimpse of the person you were meant to be. You do something selfless or inspirational. Or, you let something go. Moving forward is a constant.

Sometimes this is unexplored territory. There is no map. There is no compass. Keep your mind open and receptive. Seize the moment.

Standing up for what you think is right is usually the right thing to do. However, sitting down and listening to another person's perspective is also the right thing to do.

You can be defeated without losing your faith. It is only temporary. Many battles are lost before the war is one.

"You must have tact. The art of convincing people they know more than you." [16] (R. Mortimer,Gilbert)

START WITH EMPATHY – NEW WAVE LEADERSHIP

During this phase the leaders and subordinates bend over backwards to accommodate one another. Most people involved try to be complimentary of others. They speak optimistically about the future. They do their best to be friendly and to become friends and or respected. The goals are to establish him or her as part of the team, and to carve out and secure their position on the team. Ultimately becoming a trusted confidant whether you are a leader or a follower is the objective. This is "new wave" leadership.

"To handle yourself, use your head; to handle others, use your heart." [17]

---

[16] Ibid-2,
[17] Ibid-1, p. 57

LEADERSHIP AT ITS CORE IS GIVING, NOT GETTING

Within organizations the actions good leaders should take are rarely obvious. The core of good leadership stems from giving, not getting. To get success leaders must help those around him/her to become successful. To gain respect and happiness in the organization, leaders must give it to others. To keep joy and respect it must spread throughout the organization. To optimize results, you must have fun. Service should be fun.

"Aim for service, not success, and success will follow."[18]

[18]Ibid-1, p.225

designed by freepik.com

"There are two ways to be clever. First, think of a bright remark in time to say it. Second, think of it in time not to say it." [19]

---

[19] Ibid-1, p.227

LEADERSHIP: THE ULTIMATE MULTI-TASK

Leadership has to know who they can trust. They are trying to identify essential functions versus those that may not be as necessary. Leaders are trying to establish and re-establish their reputation and the impressions they leave. At the same time leaders have to understand who knows what, where, and when in the organization. They have to establish quick wins on a regular basis. They have to listen intently, be inclusive to the extent possible, sift-through information to get an initial understanding of the various agenda or factions that exist throughout the organization. Know the factions.

FACTIONS WITH UNDERLYING INTERESTS

There will always be factions whose agenda or interests are more important to them than the short or long term best interests of the organization. We know just by looking around our society that leaders do not have all the answers. However, leaders throughout our organizations must be willing to listen to the questions. They must be open to the reality that may be the best answer is not the answer he or she wants to hear. Use the best answer. Give credit where the credit belongs, but watch out for factions..

"People will know you are serious when you produce." (Muhammad Ali)[20]

I AM YOUR NEW LEADER

Leadership must be demonstrated, not announced. Some people are leaders without even knowing it. They can influence a decision with only a word or a look, a kind of expression, a gesture, a helping hand. Leadership takes the impossible and makes it a practical reality. Leadership is more of an internal challenge than an external challenge.

---

[20] Ibid-1, p. 3

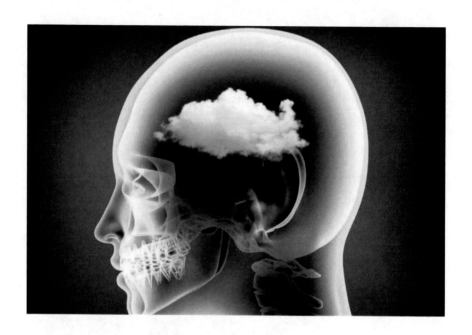

What do your employees really want? Is it respect? Is it appreciation? Is it freedom? Might it be power prestige and money?

"If you want employees to be happy, set a goal that commands their thoughts, liberates their energy, and inspires their hopes." (Andrew Carnegie) Leaders have to understand what these things are. The answers are different for different people.

LEGACY OF LEADERSHIP

The legacy of good leadership is not to be remembered, but to prepare the organization to move forward even after the current leadership is gone. As you develop your employees, they should eventually be better leaders than you.

One measure is to be clear about your vision for the organization. Then, ask yourself, "Are you moving the organization closer to the dream every day?" If the answer is "no" you have to change something. If the answer is "yes" you still will have to change something eventually.

You may take two steps forward and one step backward occasionally.

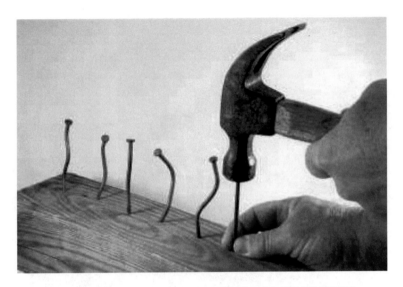

THERE ARE ALWAYS LESSONS TO BE LEARNED

For better or worse, whether good nor bad your past does not determine your future as long as lessons continue to be learned. You should be reasonably aware of your strengths, weaknesses, challenges and shortcomings. But, they do not necessarily define who you are.

Listen-Learn-Act

Barack Obama has said, "The future is ours to win. Leadership has to take us there."

Even with our shortcomings our future can be greater than our past. Change should reflect progress.

Finish what you started. Finish the job even if you have to change some of the goals.

THE MEASURE OF GREATNESS IS GOODNESS

Leadership is increasingly complex and jobs in leadership are increasingly mobile and short-lived. However, one of God's promises is: "weeping may endure for a night, but joy comes in the morning."

"There is no future in any job. The future lies with the people who hold the jobs.[21]

---

[21] Ibid-1, p.223

BUILT TO LAST

Organizations are not "built to last" any more. The changes in technology alone make this nearly impossible. Tomorrow's success depends on today's investments in leadership. Investments are necessary in leadership like never before. Organizations should not be "built to last," they should be "built to change." Leadership is the key to preeminence. It is the most important factor in energizing, engaging and creating synergy amongst the masses. It is not your father's leadership style. Its "new wave leadership." Its "liberation leadership."

LEADERS SHOULD EMBODY THE ORGANIZATION'S IDENTITY

Leaders should embody the identity of their organization. As is the case in most complex organizations there are many challenges to overcome and opportunities to seize. The act of moving the institution forward while tightly managing its scarce resources is more than ever. The competitive nature of industry, government, nonprofit agencies and educational entities is ever present. Multi-tasking is critical. While maintaining efficient and effective use of resources, good leaders should intermittently plot short and long term courses for success.

Additionally, take a look at where the "center" of your organization is. As a leader, where do you spend most of your time and attention? You may need to make some adjustments. Beware and be aware.

THE WINDS OF CHANGE ARE CONTINUOUS IMPROVEMENT

The winds of change are always swirling particularly in the midst of economic downturns, violence, tragedies and other unexpected occurrences.

The key to continuously improving our organizations is leadership. The key to affecting our trade deficit reduction is leadership. The key to making our government more effective and efficient is leadership. For us to change our society none of these things can happen in a vacuum. Ultimately, each sector needs to work with the others to improve on how our society works. Not just the leadership is necessary, but the leadership team is necessary. "New wave leadership or liberation leadership."

WHAT GOOD LEADERSHIP IS OR IS NOT

Leaders in this new millennium have new challenges. What good leadership is or is not has evolved. Today a new type of leadership is necessary as organizations try to create and re-create centers of excellence. Leadership will be the engine that drives continuous improvement. The better leaders want to help as many people as possible. When leaders are focused on service, they become more dynamic and harder to resist.

Benjamin Franklin believed that the measure of a person's greatness was the person's goodness. This is true of leaders as well. The greatest leaders cannot be great without being good. They are liberated leaders.

THE LEADERSHIP CHALLENGE

One leadership challenge in virtually all organizations is to move swiftly to eradicate negativity, complacency and mediocrity. There are new ways to approach old leadership subjects. Enjoying what you do, selfless service and putting others first are changing the guidelines for leadership. A good leader can also be your friend.

Giving people an opportunity is what leadership is about. In the middle 1800s William Thomson, a scientist, said, "Radio has no future. Don't waste your time with that. It will never go anywhere." Leadership and creativity took over and radio is where it is today. Give your people a chance. Put them in positions where they can stretch and optimize their success.

"I have no particular talent; I am merely extremely inquisitive." (Albert Einstein)[22]

---

[22] Ibid-1, p.47

DECEIT, HYPOCRISY, FEAR, INSECURITY

Much of the trouble in today's organizations stems from deceit, hypocrisy, fear and insecurity. When you experience it in your organization it is very difficult to overcome. Leaders cannot ignore the existence of these things for their employees will not ignore them. Sometimes these issues arise with leaders, at other times, these issues are created by members of the "team." Most people cannot be fooled consistently. Once they experience one or more of these attributes from leadership, individual and organizational behavior is effected for a long time to come. Sometimes a leader can pull together a quick fix, but it usually doesn't last. Every bump, bruise or challenge in these areas should be addressed as a family. When the organization is underdeveloped in these areas an analysis of individual behavior is warranted. These types of issues have to be handled one person at a time.

IT IS EASY TO BE ANGRY

We have plenty of reasons not to be happy or satisfied in our organizations. There are plenty of reasons to be unhappy, irritated or angry. After all, look at how you have been treated. It is easy to be angry at anything or anyone. It is difficult to let the anger go. It is difficult to embrace your adversaries. Paraphrasing Robert Frost, "Leadership is the ability to listen to almost anything without losing your temper or your self-confidence." [23]

---

[23] Ibid-1, p. 53

THE HARDEST THING IN AN ORGANIZATION IS FOR INDIVIDUALS AND UNITS WITHIN THE ORGANIZATION, NOT TO FEAR THE SUCCESS OF ANOTHER UNIT OR INDIVIDUAL WITHIN THE ORGANIZATION.

OPENNESS, VULNERABILITY, BUT PRIVACY HAS ITS PLACE

How vulnerable should you be as a leader? Understanding your coworkers is one thing, having them understand you is quite different. Is kindness often mistaken for weakness? Being transparent is a risk. And if you don't have the right people in the right places, or the values of some employees are in conflict with the culture you are trying to create, then, there may be a problem.

Openness and by default vulnerability is a requirement of organizational success. Privacy in an organization has its place. However, excessive privacy or secrecy spawns isolation. What leaders need is collective power, not individual power. Collective power requires collective knowledge.

Good leaders don't isolate themselves, and they don't deliberately keep people in the dark. They don't pit one person against another. Good leaders inform their coworkers and include them in the decision-making process when possible. If you are serious about being a leader and serving others, open up. Let people know who you are and what you believe.[24]

Being transparent and open is part of generously giving to the organization. Giving includes your spirit and your energy. When you give to the organizational effectiveness and efficiency, there should not be an expectation of an individual return. However, the return usually comes anyway. "Liberation Leadership."

---

[24] . "The Word for You Today." (2016)   Enon Baptist Church. December, January, February. Chester, VA. p. 45.

INDIVIDUAL SUCCESS IS EMPTY. LEADERS ARE RARELY SELF-SUFFICIENT

Succeeding alone is not as much fun as succeeding in a group.

GIVERS VERSUS TAKERS

Are you a taker or a giver? Are you motivated by your image, approval, prestige. Regardless of the talent you have, if you are motivated in these ways, among others, you may be a taker. Leadership coach Dan Reiland observes: "If communicators teach out of need and insecurity of others or even a responsibility to others, they are givers. The needy person wants praise, something the audience must give. The egotistical person wants to be lifted up, to be superior and just a little bit better than everyone else something the audience must give. Even the person motivated by responsibility wants to be seen as being responsible. Many communicators teach in one of these modes all the time and aren't aware of it. He or she may be a taker. Then there is the giver. This person teaches out of love, grace, gratitude, compassion and passion. These are giving modes. In each of these modes the audience doesn't have to give anything. The audience only has to receive. The teaching, then, becomes a gift. It fills and renews regularly."[25]

---

[25] The Word, Dec-Feb 2014, p.39

ARROGANCE AND EGOS

Arrogance seldom works to the advantage of a leader. Egos still seem to get in the way sometime. We don't always have to be better than the person next to us. Organizations exist because of the need for a system, not because of the individual. Organizations work because people listen to each other and learn from each other creating a synergy in the organization that would not exist otherwise.

What attitude do you bring to the organization? There are no menial jobs, only menial attitudes.

(William Bennett, writer, Gilbert)

POWER AND STATUS

Power and status are important in our society. Some people crave attention and they compare the attention they receive to the attention given to others. People want to feel important. They want to stand out from the crowd. People in our society push their way to the top whether it's social, financial, or through prestige. Within the context of an organization for some people this is the only opportunity to achieve. Many organizational problems could be solved if we could eliminate selfishness.

"Many organizations would be a better place if the power of love replaced some people's love of power. "[26]

---

[26] Ibid-1, p.145

SELFLESS SERVICE

In a society that promotes and supports power, I suggest that selfless service is where authentic power comes from in an organization. Real power exists in the long term for those that do not seek it or do not revel in it. For many, this way of thinking may be counter intuitive.

LEADERS PROVIDE VALUE

How important is it for people to know who you are? Leadership is not about being acknowledged, although occasionally it can be nice. Success for anyone is not about being acknowledged. Craving attention is not part of leadership. A pat on the back is not a bad thing, but growing to expect it, is. Being a good leader is not a popularity contest although good genuine leaders are often revered. Everyone in the organization has significance. A leader knows if he or she is providing value. The since of worth should predominantly come from within.

External validation or acknowledgement, if any, should come from people you trust. We are all precious commodities in our own right. If you show up every day and serve selflessly, you are on your way to being good. When you are on your way to being good, you are on your way to being great.

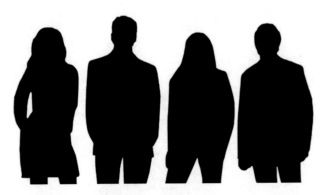

MANY OF THE BEST LEADERS IN THE WORLD TODAY ARE UNKNOWN EVEN TO THEIR PEERS. IN SOME CASES THEY MAY BE GONE BEFORE THE TRUE BENEFITS OF THEIR LEADERSHIP ARE REAPED.

ORGANIZATIONS ARE PUZZLES IN WHICH THE RIGHT PIECES HAVE TO FIT INTO THE RIGHT PLACES.

SEARCH FOR YOUR CALLING

We should not be searching for significance, we should be searching for our calling and fulfillment. Our significance exists because we are here. Our existence makes us significant. Each of us is unique and each of us has an organizational contribution to make. Everyone contributes to the organizational bottom line.

However, catching a glimpse of your self-worth is not a bad thing. Holding on to that glimpse can be.

Good leaders know what they want. They know what kind of culture they are in and what kind of culture they are seeking. The difficulty often includes the time frame and whether or not the organization is ready. The cultural vision may or may not be achievable in a given timeframe. If this vision is not achievable in a given timeframe, do not give up. It can still happen.

Integrity

The World is watching

DO THE RIGHT THING

Good leaders today should have a "quiet" sense of what is right. A reputation for always trying to do the right thing is hard to come by.

Remember; being defeated, beaten up, or losing is only a temporary state. Shake it off, re-group, assess the situation and move forward. Soon, you will be back on top.

Friendship often ends in love; but love in friendship – never.

FORTITUDE, FRIENDSHIP, FULFILLMENT

Leaders today need fortitude, friendship and fulfillment. Fortitude is when you are one step ahead of your teammates as you guide and support them as you move through the organizational objectives. Friendship is a combination of respect and loyalty. Oprah Winfrey once put it this way; "Lots of people want to ride with you in the limousine, but what you want are the people who will take the bus with you when the limousine breaks down. Fulfillment is being passionate about your cause and learning every step of the way through your journey.

THE ROLE OF PASSION IN YOUR CRUSADE

Leaders are strategists, negotiators, consensus builders, recruiters, ethicists and clairvoyants. Leaders are all things to a lot of people. The role of leadership is to give others a push. Just as parents push children on a swing, children then begin pumping themselves. People begin to challenge themselves. The success of a leader is contingent upon all the people around him or her. Do not be afraid to use your subordinates. Their perspective is often different and extremely valuable.

Leaders are pulled in different directions. They are expected to be good at what they do. Leadership is not expected to be on-the-job training although the better leaders are always learning. They are expected to get results. The results being sought depend on the constituent group.

Passion and faith drive results.

GIVE TEAM MEMBERS A PUSH, THEY WILL SOON BE PUSHING THEMSELVES.

COMMUNICATION IS HARD

Communicating with people is hard work. It takes a tremendous amount of energy to listen, understand and reason with people. People appreciate it when you try to understand their point of view. At any given point in time almost everyone in an organization is wrestling with a fear or ready to fight a battle. Understanding and knowing your colleagues can alleviate fear or fights.

Listen, Listen, Listen. Listen, Learn, Act.

LEADERS ARE NOT IN A PRIVATE CLUB

Remnants of leadership are found throughout the organization. Custodians, maintenance persons, secretaries, among others, all provide leadership. All play a role in moving the organization forward. As a leader in the structure of an organization you never know where your next lesson will come from.

All employees have a job to do that they must do well. Excellence should be expected from the person you sit next to everyday. The fundamentals in the organization should almost be automatic and should be consistently done with excellence. Employees should take pride in their work, but it should not stop there. To a certain extent, everyone in the organization should think strategically about his or her work, or unit. Organizations that rise to the top of their industry will be organizations that use their collective brainpower better.

Leaders come from every walk of life.

COMFORTABLE IN YOUR OWN SKIN

For organizations to become great, leaders have to get people to talk to each other, particularly, across departmental lines. For this to work, employees need to be secure in their job and comfortable in their own "skin."

"How can I help." "What do you think?" These are phrases good leaders use regularly.

YOUR PURPOSE

Everyone in the organization has a purpose. Purpose is led by spirit, passion and faith. Guidance, advice and support are what leaders should provide. Albeit there are various levels of emotional and functional maturity in an organization, there are still some things leaders should keep their hands off in an organization. Keeping hands off is not easy, especially when you know the right way to do things. Sometimes leaders have to let go. Leadership takes patience, discipline, civility and hard work. Leaders must consistently work on establishing and re-establishing their own purpose in the organization.

Employees cannot always optimize their potential on their own. They need help from the leadership.

Leaders should strive to know everyone's behavior in their inner circle and sometimes beyond. Hopefully, they can begin to understand it. It is easy to obsess over the behavior of others. The key word is obsess. What leaders must do, however, is to continuously focus on themselves. Somehow, leaders have to move toward fearing less and trusting more. It is what it is!

We need leaders at every level.

THE IMAGERY OF LEADERSHIP

Even the best leaders have to keep their egos in check. I have transformed a letter originally written by Calvin Miller in the "Empowered Communicator." The leadership problem is described below.

Dear supervisor, your ego has become a wall between yourself and your employees. You are not really concerned about us are you? You are mostly concerned about whether or not your concepts and ideas are working, about whether or not others think you are doing a good job. You are really afraid that you will not be applauded when you have reached goals. You are afraid that we don't understand how difficult your job is as you present emotional anecdotes to us. You're so caught up in the issue of how you are being received as a leader by those that count to you, you have not thought much about the rest of us at all. We liked you early on, but you have become so caught up in self-promotion and preservation, this becomes more important than the needs and wants of others. If we don't give you our attention, its because we feel inadequate. When you interact with us, the most important things seem to be about your next meeting. Or, is your department impeccable? Is your phraseology perfect? You seem to control everything, but us. This blindness to us is making us deaf to you. When your arrogance has been reckoned with, then there will be room for all of us in your world. Then, you will not care if we applaud your brilliance. You will be one of us.[27]

Good leaders accelerate the crusade for doing right. However, there is always a price to pay.

Good Leaders accelerate their crusade to be helpful!

[27] The Word for You Today, Good Shephard, Dec-Jan 2015, p.45

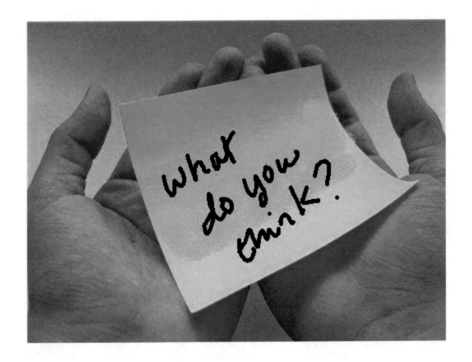

ADJUSTABLE ASSUMPTIONS

How we train and cultivate leaders is at a crossroad. Future leaders not only have to champion their cause, but they must also understand the interests of others. The others are internal and external to the organization. Self-centered leadership will not work in the long term. Future leaders have to embrace transparency. They should have no problem being a follower occasionally. Future leaders need to be "comfortable and secure in their own skin."

To serve organizations effectively leaders must be in touch with employee needs and perceptions. Here is a quick story about assumptions.

A lady in an airport lounge brought a packet of cookies and sat down to read the newspaper.

She heard a rustling noise and looked up to see the man beside her helping himself to some cookies. Not wanting to make a scene she leaned over and took one herself, hoping he would get the message. The she heard more rustling. She couldn't believe it. The man was helping himself to another cookie! There was only one left. She watched in disbelief as he broke the remaining cookie in two pushed half across to he, popped the other half in his mouth, and left. She was still furious when her flight was announced. Imagine how she felt when she opened her handbag to get her ticket out and found her unopened packet of cookies! Now, be honest, didn't you assume the stranger was helping himself to her cookies? Too often we are guilty of making assumptions about people. And, once you put someone in a box, it is hard to think of them in any other way.[28]

NO SUCH THING AS A TYPICAL LEADER

Developing leaders in critical. There is an abundance of talent. The leadership skill set for the future is different than the skill set for today. In addition to being seen and heard, future leaders have to be touched. They have to be able to turn leadership on and turn leadership off.

There is no such thing as the typical leader. There are changes in leadership needs or leadership style within the same organization. If you think you know what type of leadership works in an organization, keep thinking. Even within the same organization, there is a need for a leadership model change from time to time.

Leaders into the future will have a variety of stakeholders, each with different interest and expectations. They are expected to be more accountable, more transparent and to get better results. The results sought depend on who the stakeholder is. Everyone is not going to be happy, but at a certain level you should

---

[28] The Word 2014, p. 35

get close. If a leader cannot be all things to all people, he/she better have a team that can.

GOOD LEADERS CHANGE LIVES

Good leaders change lives. They are committed to their cause and a large part of their cause is doing what is best for the people. They can create a new organizational day every day. Paraphrasing George Washington Carver as he spoke about life in general, "I would say that the better leaders can be tender with the young, compassionate with the aged, sympathetic with the striving, and tolerant of the weak." [29] They should improve the work life of their colleagues, provide the framework from which colleagues can grow, provide a shoulder upon which colleagues can lean and provide a sanctuary where colleagues can be re-energized.

Leaders in the future cannot approach leadership in the same way. The principles of leadership are different. The expectations for leaders from our employees are different. Good leaders know when to "ride the horse in the direction it is going, or not."

Whether you are new or you have been in the organization for a number of years, individuals must constantly try to understand the environment. The environment evolves. The core variables in the environment are the personalities that exist. What are the new personalities like? Have the old personalities changed in one way or another? How can you best work with the people? Everyone is different. Everyone has a different perspective. Are the older personalities having an effect

---

[29] Ibid-2, p. 45

on the newer personalities in the organization or vice versa. How entrenched are the personalities into the culture?

Organizational behavior has to do with the perspective and perception of the individuals.

UNDERSTAND THE CULTURE

Understanding the culture of the organization is extremely important to providing any sort of guidance. Observe how people treat each other. The inside forces are the greatest challenge. Leaders should know the internal as well as the external battles. Bumps in the road usually create tremendous opportunities for success. Handling the internal obstacles is a key to success. This is the test.

Many people get tired, get frustrated or become depressed. Even the best of leaders have moments when dropping out seems like the thing to do. However, patience and introspective thought provides fresh strength. Leaders with the best of reputations stumble and fall occasionally. But those who wait as they gather their thoughts, and those that are true to themselves and others come back bigger, better and stronger than ever. As leaders rise above their micro level issues and look at their environment from a broader perspective. Leaders who are not able to look at their situation from a broader perspective will not be able to refresh their minds and restore their energy. Leaders must aim to serve and also be true to themselves regardless of the circumstances.

BIG BROTHER IS WATCHING

During this information age, leaders are being watched all the time. It's not always how you handle successes that is important, it is how you handle the losses, the grief, the disappointment, and the failures. This is what is important. Additionally, various audiences will be watching how you treat your 'subordinates,' your enemies and even your family members. In today's world you can be sure that your light shines everywhere. The light also shines in many places for which you are not aware.

FILL IN THE LEADERSHIP GAPS

Leadership does not always demand its own way. Leaders do not have to control or micromanage every aspect of the organization. Good leaders guide, they do not control. Make the good ideas those of the employees.

Leaders and their colleagues have to look for common ground. Is it possible to work together and be true thine self? Is there a difference between being accommodating and being versatile? Can you be versatile without being phony? The leader cannot be all things to all people but he or she has to have someone on staff that can fill the gaps.

ON THE SAME PAGE?

Leaders and their colleagues should be saying the same thing to all constituents. If different people get different messages from leadership throughout the organization, a problem exists. Everyone in the organization has a purpose.

At some point, everyone's purpose must genuinely intersect.

CIVILITY

The social, political and economic environment around the world make civility in leadership more challenging. In leading organizations around the world, caring and sensitive leaders are needed. The masses may not understand this. They want strong powerful leaders. They want leaders that will fight for them. They may mistake kindness for weakness. In the long term all these attributes are critical for having civility. It is not what you do, it is how you do it. These attributes are not mutually exclusive. All these attributes can be used in the context of civility. For leadership to be better than it's ever been, civility should be a constant.

EVERYONE HAS HAD ISSUES WITH LEADERS OR LEADERSHIP

Organizations have issues because the people in them have issues. Within the organization and perhaps outside employees have experienced rejection or abuse. At some point we have all been disappointed.

For this reason it is important that leaders provide access and opportunity to those they work with. Leaders should be engines that drive succession planning. The framework from which future leaders will grow will include open-mindedness, humility and vision. Lessons to be learned, then, become front and center when leaders are open-minded, humble and have vision.

GOOD LEADERS ARE COMPLEX YET SIMPLE

Is a good leader complex or simple. Perhaps he or she is both. The difficulty stems from each individual being able to own up to strengths and weaknesses. If individual leaders decide to give into the societal and/or organizational culture that exists, at least make the decision in a conscientious way. Identify your strengths and weaknesses, then come up with a plan.

As you implement the plan lead with a smile.

COMMUNICATION: HIERARCHICAL, DIAGONAL, HORIZONTAL

These are exciting times for organizational development. People are craving transparency. Ideas are being shared. Data is becoming more available. Suggestions are coming from different departments in and outside organizations. There is significant forward movement in the building or renovation of facilities. Infrastructure and logistics are being discussed at every turn. Technology is changing organizational vision constantly. In many organizations forward thinkers are alive and well, and are becoming less encumbered. There are dynamic organizations in every sector.

Organizational planning and leadership occurs at many levels, covers multiple timeframes and is a very iterative process. Input from every segment of the organization should drive the planning efforts. Some organizations have made significant gains in their continuous pursuit of excellence. They have implemented processes that encourage assessment, review and change. They have rewarded and recognized employees for their thoughtfulness and willingness to change.

Put yourself in the shoes of your colleagues. What incentives are appropriate? What rewards are necessary?

The better organizations thrive on having productive and congenial environments. Awards are being given for implementation of the most creative idea. All units have open meetings with the CEO. Awards for the best team contribution are given. And, a number of social events are planned throughout the year. It is important for leaders to demonstrate their interest in the work experience of their employees. The quality of organizational life for each employee should be an objective of many organizations.

Leadership is responsible for building relationships with and encouraging participation from internal and external constituencies. The different insights and perspectives allow for better decisions to be made in the long term.

YOUR TEAM; THEY ARE NEVER PERFECT

Creating your team is extremely important, but first and foremost you have to feel good about your mission. All kinds of communication are necessary in creating the team. The mission of the organization and each individual's purpose should be front and center. Values also have to be clear. Speak openly about trust, management style and loyalty before they become issues. Truth, honesty and commitment are part of this. Expectations are then established. They may evolve, but they are ongoing.

In creating your team the rules of engagement become important. No leader requires people to act in a certain way. However, leadership should indicate that they will not embarrass individuals or belittle them. We will not speak ill of you in public. We do not expect you to always agree, but we do expect you to yield to the will of the team. The public perception should be that we are a team and we are all moving together.

PERFECTLY HONEST

People are never perfect so they will never be perfectly successful. However, in our society the importance of integrity has never been greater. Integrity simply means that your actions equal your words.[30] However, the challenges related to keeping your word are tremendous for well-intended, thoughtful leaders. Sometime promises are made without knowing all the consequences. Sometimes their word is given without knowing all the facts or variables. There are ways not to keep your word in the right way.

Ideally, thorough analyses has to be done. However, sometimes timelines are an issue. If decision making were easy, there would be a lot more agreement on what the decisions are. Even with the dynamics in organizations integrity should be maintained. It is possible to add to your perceived integrity by backing off a decision. Sometimes it may take more time than anticipated to fulfill a promise or to follow through on a commitment. Integrity will withstand the passage of time.

Developing a reputation for having integrity is hard. Maintaining and keeping the reputation for having integrity is harder.

The dynamics in our society and the culture in our organizations are becoming more complex. The environment in which we live and work is not going to becoming easier. We have to become better leaders.

---

[30] Ibid-1, p.114

YOUR WORK IS YOUR CAUSE

Leaders have to be integrated completely into their organizational community. For the better leaders, there work also happens to be their cause. And, somehow, they are able to turn criticism into collaboration. This takes sacrifice, particularly, a sacrifice of the ego. If your work is truly your cause, it is worth it.

When you win, nothing hurts. (Joe Namath)[31]

---

[31] Ibid-2, p.45

SPEND TIME WITH THE TEAM

When some employees begin to say they don't see you any more, it may be that you are spending too much time with a small group that is more likely to support your ideas. It is often good to spend time with your team in the presence of others in the organization. This tends to build unity throughout the organization. You still have to have the right people in the right positions.

A leader with a small group of committed people can make things happen.

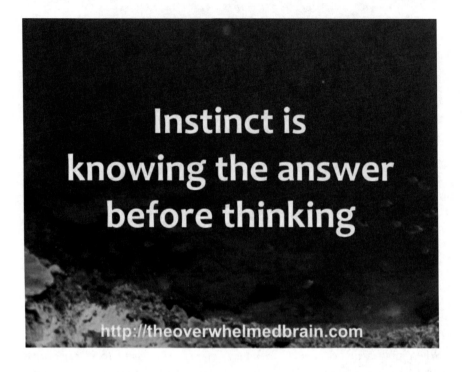

Instinct is knowing the answer before thinking

http://theoverwhelmedbrain.com

SOME LEADERS DO BETTER BY ACCIDENT, THAN THOSE WITH LEADERSHIP KNOWLEDGE DO ON PURPOSE

There are some leaders that do better by accident, than those with leadership knowledge do on purpose. If you understand your strengths and weaknesses and become true to yourself, you will enter a state of consciousness that will always be there. Unless you are willing to put the needs of your organization and the people ahead of your needs, then there is no point to becoming a leader. Eventually you will need the organization and you will need some of the people in it. Hopefully, they need you to.

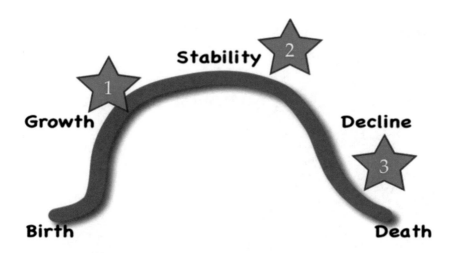

LEADERSHIP LIFE CYCLE

Leaders should be in the introduction phase of their organization's life cycle all the time. This is necessary because growth and development is not linear. Much of the time leaders take three steps forward and one step backward. The one step backward often includes working with naysayers and handling unexpected developments, among other things.

Leadership is 25% vision and 75 % history lesson.

Leaders do not start out being leaders. Leaders plod along working in the trenches as they figure out their approach and their style. However, an organization that looks backwards to often risks being left behind.

Keep the long term vision in mind, but also do not lose site of the next 100 days. Focus on your customers, your employees and be sure to declare what matters most on a regular basis.

Leadership involves taking something that already exists in the organization, the people, the materials, the instrumentation; revamp it, re-shuffle it, make modifications and move it forward. Stick together and reinforce the behaviors that are right for the long term.

ANYTHING THAT CAN BE CHANGED WILL EVENTUALLY BE CHANG

LEADERS HAVE TO WORK AT IT

For some leaders it appears that everything comes easy. Most leaders have to work at it. Leading is hard. Leading in an ethical, moral and civil way, and having others do the same is challenging. Measuring the success of leadership does not always have to be monetary it can often be measured by the triumphs over obstacles within and outside the organization.

Most good leaders have times for which they were battered during their journey. In some cases they are battered continuously. The path of even the best leaders includes steep hills and jagged rocks. The success is often just beyond the pain.

EVERYONE STUMBLES AND FALLS

No matter how good you are or how much success you have had, everyone stumbles and falls occasionally. The best leaders in the world periodically have problems in the organization some of which are quite serious. At any given point in time there is a need for everyone to reflect, be pensive and be refreshed. Organizational life takes a lot of energy. The pressures and the pace can drain anyone. What organizational life takes out of you has to be periodically restored. Once refreshed, good leaders begin to soar once again. With good leaders who are also good people, this can happen time and time again.

Be more concerned about your character than your reputation, because your character is what you really are, while your reputation is merely what others think of you. (John Wooden)[32]

THE ROAD TO SUCCESS

The difficulties, hardships and trials of organizations and leaders within the organizations are actually the road to success. Peril is the element from which leadership is developed. Success is often an idea away. Many times leaders quit, are removed or are fired before that next idea puts the organization over the top. There is a fine line between staying with a direction too long, or, not staying with a direction long enough.

---

32 Ibid-2, p.37

THE FIGHT IS FROM WITHIN

The challenge leaders have is not with their competition in business, the opposing political party, or being first to the market with a new product. The fight/challenge is with any stronghold that keeps individuals and the organization from reaching its potential. The fight is with internal or external people that attempt to hold individuals or the organization back. Power silos within the organization have to give way to what is best for the entire organization.

If there is anything to be changed in the organization, first examine whether something should be changed in the leadership.

THE TIME FOR CHANGE

Any time may or may not be the right time to start an initiative. The questions tend to be; do you have the right people in the right places? If you do not, can you change this in a timely manner? Do you have the other resources you need including support from the right stakeholders. For example, when polls show that two-thirds of the American people don't like math or science and your goal is to increase the number of scientists and mathematicians, there is a challenge.

Management by intimidation is more mainstream than many people might think. There are a few in every organization. They still get results, albeit, usually short term results. Don't toss out your values.

SABOTAGE FROM THE INSIDE

Many organizations need more people to point out what is right with the organization and less people to harp on what is wrong. Some organizations have a cadre of people who spend their time figuring out what is wrong and devise ways to promote what is wrong. This is how they spend their time. This is not time well spent.

THREE COMMON PROBLEMS

Three kinds of problems prevent organizations from achieving their goals and otherwise optimizing their existence.

1. People who have other interests or other agenda. Some people have egos. Some are jealous of others. Others may be insecure and wonder who is going to get credit.
2. Some people are in the unit in name only. They may be takers and not givers. They want all the privileges, but none of the responsibilities. They will go along for the ride as long as, if there are any changes, the changes do not impact them in a negative way.
3. There are people that work against the unit. These people tend to be antagonistic and have opinions that are counter to the direction of the organization. For many of these people dissention is an end in and of itself.
4. In some cases the individuals may truly believe in moving in a different direction and do not want to control their actions.

PULL TOGETHER OR GET PULLED APART

For the most part people and leadership either pull the organization together, or pull the organization apart. Oftentimes there is no middle ground. Every organizational bump bruise or challenge should be addressed as an organizational family whenever possible.

In the middle 1800's William Thomson, a scientist said, "Radio has no future. Don't waste your time with that. It will never go anywhere."

Sometimes there are people high in your organization that denounce the vision. Sometimes people in the organization will toss firecrackers under the seat of the colleague that sits next to him or her. Some organizations have people that spend their time working against another person or persons in the organization rather than working with the leaders. Leaders have to know and understand the goals of each individual on the team whether the goal is overt or covert. Then the leader has to make decisions on who the teammates should be. Even the greatest leaders run across issues like sabotage, internal strife or differences in values. Sometimes battles are won by the other side, but they cannot win the war.

There are roadblocks everywhere.

As a leader you never know what or who is around the next corner.

Disagreements and differences of opinion will happen in any unit or organization. It's how they respond to disagreements that separates the better leaders from others. One of the difficult challenges is to adequately and tactfully watch the actions and the reactions of your colleagues. The first thing to do is to be present.

We regret the inconvenience of doing the right things, but…

TEMPER, TEMPER

Good listeners have the ability to listen to anything without losing their temper or losing self confidence. Incidently, there may be a point at which losing your temper is a good thing. Leaders that are good listeners tend to be popular everywhere. Good listeners acknowledge and show appreciation for everything that is done for them or the organization no matter how large or how small.

What do you mean, we don't communicate! Revenge never works in the long term.

Tit for Tat = 0

THE PERCEPTION OF LEADERSHIP

People throughout any organization talk about what they perceive, what they heard, or what they think they know. People tend to talk about others in the organization, some of whom they know and some of whom they do not know. Perceptions of leadership, departments, units and colleagues are established, re-established and sometimes reinvented. Facts may or may not be relevant.

How leadership responds to disagreement is crucial. Do you take offense? Do you shoot the messenger? Do you feel that your employees do not understand the circumstance or don't understand you? The reaction of leadership should be tempered. As long as the people you are listening to want the best for you and your organization, everything is "good". The problems arise when people do not have the same agenda. Disagreements help to discipline us. Everyone should be committed to the truth. There is something in each of us that would rather look good, than be good.

MISCONCEPTIONS

Being busy is not the same as taking action!

Being smart is only one element of leadership.

Even if you have the right to do something, this does not mean that you should do it.

Even if you do nothing, it must be viewed as a tactical or strategic action. There must be a purpose.

Sometimes no action is the best action.

HOPE

Even in today's information age there are many employees in organizations that have lost their feeling of hope for themselves. There is an absence of value, purpose and worthiness. People in our organizations have the same issues that are present in our communities. Their relationships are having difficulties, their jobs have no future, there is no dream, and no emotional confidence. Can these people be brought to life? Can they live their work life to the fullest extent. Leadership is not just about the leader.

THE MISSION IS BIGGER THAN YOU.

Some employees are incapable of thinking beyond their own needs. Sometimes they cannot think past their current issue. They and others may have their own agenda. Their mental condition makes it impossible for them to think in a broader more abstract way. It often takes more than one visionary to move these individuals forward. It often needs to be a team effort among those that have the wherewithal. It takes a team to move some employees forward. Organizational synergy can work miracles and sometimes it takes miracles. Look for the leaders among the masses. These people will do a lot of heavy lifting. If at first you don't succeed, you are about average.

Individuals are assessing their value in the organization and are positioning themselves for that value. They are also directly or indirectly positioning others through conversation throughout the organization.

FACT AND FICTION

This happens in organizations for better or for worse, in fact or in fiction. Perceptions and in some cases rumors can "take legs.

One day an eight year old boy went to the pet store with his dad to buy a puppy. The store manager showed then to a pen where five little furry puppies were huddled together. After a while the boy noticed one of the litter all by itself in an adjacent pen. The boy asked, "Why is that puppy alone." The manager explained, "That puppy was born with a bad leg and would be crippled for the rest of his life, so we are going to have to put him to sleep." "You are going to kill this puppy?" the boy said sadly while patting it. "You have to realize that this puppy would never be able to run and play with a boy like you." After a short conversation with his boy, the dad told the manager that they wanted to buy the puppy with the bad leg. The store owner said, "For the same amount of money you could have one of the healthy ones. Why do you want this one?" To answer the manager's question the boy bent over and pulled up the pants on his right leg. He exposed the brace beneath and said, "Mister, I want this one because I understand what he is going through." [33]

Leaders should know what their colleagues and competitors are going through.

---

[33] Ibid-1, p. 157,158

WHO IS YOUR LEADER

However, there is something to be learned from everyone in the organization. Never downplay the importance of anyone in the organization. Sometimes all leaders have to do is expose their colleagues to the light and nurture them consistently. They will then take responsibility. Engage employees and challenge them intellectually. Challenge their views.

You get the best effort from others by not lighting a fire beneath them, but by building a fire within them. (Bob Wilson)[34] You have to build the right kind of fire. Success by any means possible is not good, and it's not usually long lasting. The fire needs to include openness, honesty, empathy and selflessness. The key is to light this fire within each individual in the organization in a similar way. It is labor intense, but certainly attainable. This ensures that any changes that occur are more likely to be long term. Changes.

Vertical responsibilities in the organization are obviously important, but the horizontal responsibilities are also important. Horizontal responsibilities enable us to build the organizational framework.

When individuals in the organization volunteer to do the work in regards to an initiative or a change, leadership is displayed. Perhaps it is passion, perhaps its drive, perhaps its curiosity; whatever it is that moves the individual to volunteer may not matter. Volunteering usually means that they want to do it. Doing

---

[34] Ibid-2,p.161

additional work outside the normal domain is leadership. Doing more than is expected is also leadership.

WHEN THE GOING GETS TOUGH......

As a leader everything is not going to work out the way you would like it to all the time. When you are depressed, do something for someone else. [35]

As people mature into their various leadership roles, they begin to find out what type of leader they are and what type of leader they will never be.

The benefits and shortcomings of "staying in your lane" are numerous.

Few leaders actually know what they mean when they say that they love their organization. Love means they have total unrelenting interest in their organization. The price leaders have to pay includes making their self-interest at third or fourth priority. They may not see eye to eye, but they can still walk in unison with their supervisors and subordinates.

---

[35] Buettner,2012 p.145

It was John Kennedy that said, "When written in Chinese, the word 'crisis' is composed of two characters. One character represents danger and the other character represents opportunity." Good leaders have this approach. When the truly gut-wrenching decisions have to be made, the opportunities for change can be seized. The visionary leaders can think through these opportunities that may not exist otherwise.

LEADERSHIP NONNEGOTIABLES

-Become generally interested in your employees.

-Be a good listener and talk in terms of the other person's interest.

-Make the other person feel important

(Dale Carnegie)[36]

---

[36] Ibid-2, p.137

THE MOST VALUABLE PLAYER

The CEO of a company summoned one of his VP's. He said, I want you to fire that woman in the office down the hall. I have been watching her for the past two weeks and all I have seen her do is look out the window. Wait a minute, the vice president said, that's the department head that created our innovative global supply chain system. She is the one responsible for increasing sales to countries in Asia by 30% and she is responsible for our new positive relationship with the Chinese government. The CEO said; She thought of all these things as she looked out the window? Then, let's get someone down here to wash her window.[37]

---

[37] Ibid-1, p. 187

LEADERSHIP IS A LIFESTYLE

Good leaders do things that most managers don't get around to. Leadership is not a single event, but a lifestyle.

In discovering or doing your life's work, it is important to come to terms with what you think is right. You may certainly think about what other people have done or what others are doing, but do not compare yourself to others. Your style is uniquely different.

In order to fill your purpose in the organization you have to understand the expectations of others. Everyone that is close to you in the organization has an expectation. Even the best leaders disappoint people with some of their decisions. Becoming the manager that others want may not always be the best way to lead. Your desire has to be to optimize the success of everyone in it. Sometimes predicting the reaction of those around you is unlikely or impossible. Everyone has an agenda whether it is overt or covert. A leadership challenge is to display the best version of who you are all the time. Ultimately you are only really happy when you are being the person you are.

" MOST OF OUR EMPLOYEES TRY TO
DRESS FOR SUCCESS...YOU, ON THE
OTHER HAND, SEEM TO BE GOING
WITH FASHION FOR FAILURE! "

WEARING THE RIGHT SUIT WILL NOT GET YOU INTO A LEADERSHIP ROLE, BUT WEARING THE WRONG SUIT WILL KEEP YOU OUT.

FIRST RATE LEADERS HIRE FIRST RATE EMPLOYEES. SECOND RATE LEADERS HIRE THIRD RATE EMPLOYEES.

VIRTUALLY EVERY POSITION IS ONE OF INFLUENCE

IN PURSUIT OF PERFECTION

-------The perfect leader is never belligerent, never late, never changes his/her mind, never absent, is always confident. The only perfect leader I could find was Bugs Bunny. Perfect people need not apply.

-------Peril is the element in which power is developed. Difficulties, hardships and trials are the road to success for the best leaders.[38] A strong sense of purpose often buffers against stress. When the purpose is exhibited, the organization has a way of helping to propel you along.

-------Leaders have enemies. Some enemies are known and others are not known. Thus, the phrases "dog eat dog' and "cut throat" exist. Not matter what is done there will be enemies on the right and on the left. You do not have to be a bad person to be hated? All good leaders are hated by somebody.

-------The world is not perfect and neither are the people in it. Leaders always need faith regardless of the circumstances they find themselves in.

-------All of this can affect your psyche. When you are down, you have to do something for yourself. Treat yourself to "happy hour." Consistency and moderation are a must.

-------Sometimes its important to go directly at issues, particularly issues that are "low hanging fruit." Early in the tenure of a new leader, the price paid may be less for tough decisions or even mistakes. On the other hand first impressions are critical as well. Leaders must be careful. The price paid may be nonrefundable, at least for the short term.

-------Immediate gratification is important, but patience is necessary for long term success. Patience helps us to learn. We are not losing time, we are gaining time through many lessons along the way. Patience enables us to correct our mistakes. There is pain along the way and patience enables us to endure the pain as we become better along the way. It allows us to better analyze who we are working with.

---

[38] Ibid-1, p. 7

The Pat on the Back!

THE STRATEGIC CHALLENGE

At some point most people not just formal leaders in an organization begin to think about what the leadership challenge is in the organization. Will any strategic change be a good thing or bad thing for me personally. When the dust settles will the changes be permanent or will they be phased out? How does my existence in the organization change. Am I able to be myself? Do I have to worry about the person next to me sabotaging my efforts. Are there more firecrackers being thrown from within the organization than from outside the organization. Am I able to trust my colleagues to have my best interest in mind or will they always fend for themselves?

Trust involves inclusiveness. Leaders need to be accessible. If they are not accessible others will become leaders by default. Listening will have to be viewed as an art and a science. The importance of teambuilding cannot be overstated especially as you nurture tomorrow's innovators.

YOU CAN'T DO IT ALONE

Today's leaders have to promote, support and implement partnerships, collaborations and consortia, internal to the organization and external to the organization. This is the new leadership. No unit can operate in a vacuum and optimally succeed. Partnerships necessitate constant dialogue, excellent interpersonal skill and trust. Existing partnerships have to be strengthened and renewed regularly while new partnerships are being considered.

LEADERSHIP IS THE NEW SUPPLY CHAIN

Leadership is the new supply chain. The supply chain is the market. Leaders that understand they are the new supply chain and do more than what is asked will never be depleted. There will always be bumps, bruises and some bleeding along the way, but values and service will prevail in the longer term.

Leaders today have to be able to change job function industries and markets quickly. All employees must have goals every year, even if the goals are not public. The organization must make the best product, deliver the best service, and work with the best people.

Timing is important. Leaders can move too quickly or too slowly. Sometimes a particular activity may not be right for a significant amount of time.

IT'S THE LITTLE THINGS

In partnering the little things matter most to the employees. Sharing benefits when you can with your partners. Providing some perks. On a college campus each unit effects the quality of education. From the custodians, to the academic advisors, to the accountants, everyone effects the quality of education offered to students.

Good leaders find areas where there are mutual benefits between organizations or units. Competition in any industry today is such that organizations will have to accomplish much more in the future than they had to accomplish in the past. Competition will be equally intense and much more diverse.

In better organizations sales personnel, finance people, groundskeepers to name a few, all provide leadership. In most instances they provide leadership not only in their own unit, but across unit boundaries. Leadership is not always provided along strict structural lines. There are usually individuals throughout the organization that provide leadership in a variety of ways.

SELF-FULFILLING PROPHECY

Set high expectations and provide incentives for employees to achieve them.

At the end of the day, goals and targets are crucial. Goals and targets can unite and inspire people with the right frame of mind. Sometime leaders and their teams hit their targets and sometimes they do not. Hitting targets is important, but what really matters is assessing why you got the results you did. The reality is that continuous improvement is what is more important.

It is possible that your vision may work out differently from what was planned. Your organization may not end up being the most prestigious organization in the region, but perhaps it fills a particular niche with a particular type of customer. You can still be the best at what you do.

If leading people by using a self-fulfilling prophecy seems easy, maybe it is, but, then again, maybe it isn't. There is often another "shoe to drop." Just because the waters are calm, doesn't mean that there aren't gators in the swamp. There is always the unexpected or the unpredicted. When you expect the unexpected, everything in the universe is predictable including failure and success.

BE TRUE TO THINE SELF

As you are true to your ideals and spirit, eventually, you will exceed all expectations and you will be a blessing for others.

When it feels like you are losing, you are actually learning.[39] When your environment knocks you down, grumbling is okay for a day or two, but beyond that it is time to move on. Have the patience to wait for the kind of experiences that will promote you and your cause in a positive way. Every experience has lessons attached, learn those lessons and move forward. Build your empire from within.

---

[39] The Word, 2012, p. 35

LEADERSHIP RULES OF THUMB

Fulfilling your leadership purpose and becoming the leader you should be, not the leader you want to be is the pursuit of excellence. Many people equate leadership success to implementing the latest leadership techniques may be helpful, but does not naturally evolve into good leadership.

-------As a leader you never know where your next lesson may come from.

-------The spirit in you gives life to your leadership.

-------Be suspicious of short term fixes to save money. The true costs of layoffs may outweigh the payroll savings to gained. Organizations have a tremendous investment in people. Be a steward of the relationships.

-------Lower the pain of staying; Treat employees with respect and dignity. Fair compensation and benefits.

LEADERSHIP PILLARS

Leaders have to embrace change, not just manage or enhance change.

Leaders have to yield and use different types of expertise that exists throughout the organization.

Must have the capacity to balance the needs and wants of all the stakeholders.

Must respond affirmatively and confidently to increasing expectations of accountability.

Must multi-task by fulfilling the traditional organizational functions of the day while meeting the new challenges of tomorrow.

He or she must operate well between the creative inclinations of the futurists and the status quo of the naysayers.

PERSONAL UNDERPINNINGS OF QUALITY LEADERS

Clear expectations.

Be flexible.

Provide development.

Give employees all the credit all the time.

Understand that it is really not all about the money.

Eliminate harassment, abuse, humiliation.

As leaders we should not pray for the massive difficulties to be removed, what we really need is the courage to remove them.[40]

---

[40] Ibid-1, p. 42

DARE TO BE DIFFERENT

Dare to be different. Doing the right things and doing them the right way may very well be different. Daring to be different is risky. Some organizations may not be ready. Some organizations may need to work on the fundamentals of doing business before it would be ready for a risk-taking leader. For many the notion of "servant leadership" is still unconventional. Understand your organization.

-------Individual wellness includes remembering the people who worked and sacrificed to give you a chance to be a leader.

------- The least you can do is be open, honest, humble and have integrity.

-------Keeping the organization focused on priorities is critical. The power of focus is huge. Focus produces purpose, and purpose produces passion.

POWER, POSITION, PRESTIGE

Leadership is not about power, position, or prestige. Leadership is about goodness, humility, service and character. The better leaders are generous, devoted and caring. Good leaders are not a particular people from a particular place. The best leaders embody the human spirit.

LEADERSHIP IS LOCAL

Leadership is local. Success relies a great deal on the ability to meet people where they are. Good leadership often requires you to act in the best interest of other people or other units. Be concerned about what is in the best interest of the whole organization. Sometimes a decision has to be made about what is in your best interest and what is in the best interest of the organization.

-------A certain amount of failure makes us better. There is a fine line between having too much failure or just enough. The kind of failure is important as well.

-------"Success is 99% failure." Sorchia Honda, Honda Corp.[41]

-------"Failure is 90% mental and the other half is attitude." Yogi Berra

-------The best leaders have failed many times before becoming successful. Making mistakes is not a bad thing. Learning from the mistakes is the issue.

---

[41] Ibid-2, p. 232

VALUE THE PEOPLE

It is fairly obvious that no leader can succeed on his or her own. But, the better leaders do not just engage others, but they value others. Seeing the value of others throughout the organization is crucial. Value must be placed on all stakeholders, internal and external. The value must be genuine. People know how you really feel about them. Many of us have to get over ourselves. We have to change our focus from being inward to being outward. [42]

Employees always ask themselves whether their supervisors care about them or not. Almost without exception the best experience employees have is when people care. Provide the shoulder on which employees can stand. Provide the sanctuary from which employees can depend. the moment a leader's attention is on service to his/her subordinates, colleagues, or superiors the leader becomes more dynamic, more forceful and harder to resist. It is hard to resist someone that is trying to help you.

The level at which you receive cooperation and support sometimes depends on the level at which you have given to the organization and the individuals within it. The return on your investment may not be immediate, it may not even be timely, but it will eventually come. Sometimes in the short term the opposite happens. Not only is there no return, but there may be angst and antagonism.

Giving in this context means empathizing, acknowledging the needs of others, being open-minded and versatile. Within the organization when you give within this context. The effect of this approach will outlive your time in the organization. It begins to create a culture change. The reputation of the organization can change for years to come.

Considering the interests of others in the organization may not always bode well for the leader. Sometimes these interests can conflict with other individual interests. The more forward thinking a leader is, the more he or she is able to see things from someone else's point of view and act or not act.

---

[42] The Word, 2016, p. 46

Me, Myself & I

SELFISH ATTITUDES IN THE ORGANIZATION

Selfish attitudes within organizations cause the demise of organizations. Leaders must not only be focused on their agenda, but also must understand the agenda of others. Good leaders must not only interact and focus on those people that are important to their agenda, but they should also be well aware of the agenda of others. There are many people that are not in the main stream, many people that may not have covert power that are important.

If it does not matter who gets the credit in an organization, the organization is usually healthier. In some ways less mature leaders may view the good ideas or activities in the following way. In his document "Property Law a Viewed by a Toddler," Michael V. Hernandez describes the world from a typical child's viewpoint. I think this applies to the ways in which some leaders view the good ideas, achievements or successes.

1. If I like it, it's mine.
2. If it is in my hand, it is mine.
3. If I can take it from you it's mine.
4. If I had it a little while ago it's is mine.
5. If it's mine, it must never appear to be yours in any way.
6. If I am doing or building something, all the pieces are mine.
7. If it looks like mine, its mine.
8. If I saw it first, its mine.
9. If I can see it, it's mine.
10. If I think it's mine, its mine.[43]

---

[43] The Word, 2015, p.45

MATURITY IN LEADERSHIP IS LEARNED! SUCCESSFUL LEADERSHIP LOOKS LIKE THIS.

-------Outcomes exist at every level.

-------Collaborative business processes are developed across units.

-------Embrace diverse ideas and thoughts.

-------Establish mechanisms for feedback within and around the organization.

-------Provide activities that promote and support teambuilding within and around the organizations

-------Have substantial dissemination of information about issues and developments effecting the unit or organization.

-------Employees become comfortable sharing their perspective.

-------Employees do not panic about an occasional failure.

-------Employees become passionate and feel good about their work.

-------Over deliver to your employees and your customers.

-------Take full advantage of the strengths of each employee.

NEW WAYS TO APPROACH OLD CHALLENGES

Leaders have to have the mind-set of the team, the unit and/or the organization first. In any industry whether it is business, government or education the team that works best together has the best outcome. In leadership you are your brother's keeper. However, you are not your brother's micro-manager.

No leaders can be all things to all people, but most leaders can do some things for many people and can delegate the other things to other people that can accomplish them. The better leaders will find new ways to approach old challenges. They should be knowledgeable, perceptive and humane. They should be secure in their self-awareness and sensitive to the needs and aspirations of others.

Leadership does not mean forcing change demanding respect and accepting credit for success with much fanfare. True change often doesn't come quickly. Respect must be earned. No great success has ever come from just one person. The Chinese philosopher Lao-Tzu said, "When the best leader's work is done, the people say, 'We did it ourselves'."

Figuring Out Future Challenges

ORGANIZATIONAL CHALLENGES OF THE COMING YEARS:

Structural deficits cannot be tolerated.

Other than people, infrastructure and logistics will be keys to success.

Must continue to invest in key priorities.

Innovation, Innovation, Innovation

If necessary, take a large cut once and factor in revenue losses as budgets are built.

When necessary corrective action plans should accompany any forecasted budget.

Take advantage of the difficult decisions that lie ahead to address your priorities.

Know your resources.

Be clear about your priorities.

Get involved with a variety of units.

Foster relationships through the organization.

Look to the future, now!

PURSUING THE VISION

Can the organization get to its vision or are the barriers and other agenda more pressing in the short term? Does the organization have to always take two steps backward, after taking three steps forward? Eventually, all good organizations get to their vision. It may just take a little more time with a few more casualties.

ENDLESS TRANSFORMATIONS

The need for endless adaptations and transformation are what leadership is all about. The legacy of a good leader is not to be remembered, but to prepare the future leaders to be better than the current ones. In many instances leaders will not get to see the fruit of their labor, but their children will see it.

Few people recognize the name Walter Hunt. Yet industrial historians consider Hunt one of the few authentic geniuses the United States has produced. Walter Hunt was an inventor and was responsible for more practical and successful inventions than any other American. Among the many inventions that flowed from his fertile mind were the fountain pen, rifle, sewing machine, paper collar, and burglar and fire alarms. Yet Hunt, born in 1796, died in poverty, practically unknown. His paper collar, first designed when cotton became scarce during the American Civil War, was laughed at. But by the beginning of the 20th century, nearly 40 years after his death, over 400 million were being worn each year in the U.S. alone.

Hunt's lockstitch sewing machine, designed in 1834, was never promoted by hunt because he feared it would put thousands of seamstresses out of work. He did not have the imagination to see that eventually it would create more jobs than it displaced. Years later, when sewing machines were being sold commercially, hunt was told it was too late for him to claim the rights to his invention. Likewise, another inventor is credited with designing the breech-loading cartridge-firing rifle. Though Hunt invented the rifle it carried the name of the man who marketed it. Winchester. Walter Hunt's brilliant mind could have made him rich and famous. Instead he died broke and disillusioned. Some say he lacked the courage of his convictions, lacked faith in himself and in his idea. However, he made a difference. He was a forward-thinking leader who was not appreciated during his time. I suspect there are plenty of leaders who are unsung or underappreciated during our time. [44]

THE ENEMY WITHIN US

In organizations today leaders have enemies. Some enemies are known and others are not known.

Throughout organizational life periodic failure is inevitable. Thinking about how things should have been is natural. Dwelling on how things should have been is not natural. It takes the same energy to bounce back from failure as it does to wallow in in.

Leaders should be just as enthusiastic about the success of their peers or colleagues as they are about their own success. Jealousy and insecurity is a difficult emotion to overcome.

BECOMING BETTER HUMAN BEINGS

"Excellence is the result of caring more than others think wise; Risking more than others think safe; Dreaming more than others think is practical; And expecting more than others think is possible." [45]

Leaders should learn new ways to solve old problems. They look at things differently. Look beyond perceived limitations and imagine things as they could be. Leadership is ultimately about helping individuals to become better human beings. Creators, pioneers and visionaries are all leaders. Do they always succeed? The answer is no.

---

[45] Ibid-2

However the legacy of good leaders is not only to get results today, but to prepare the organization for tomorrow. The most daunting task for leaders is to orchestrate an integrated web of relationships within and around the organization.

Good leaders must always stay the course with values and service. The wisdom that is gained from the best of times and from the worst of times make us the leaders we are. Their friends and their enemies have molded the leaders into who they are today. Every leader has a story to tell. Every leader has had issues. If they have not had issues, then, they are either very fortunate or they have not lived long enough.

Leaders should be asking not who is right, but what is right. Even getting at what is right is often challenging enough.

BETTER LEADERS:

--Learn from the past, but maintain spontaneity

--Lose interest in judging others unnecessarily

--Lose interest in having too much conflict

--Have frequent episode of showing appreciation

LEADERSHIP IS ACTION NOT POSITION

DOING WHAT IS RIGHT IS A CHALLENGE. DOING IT IN THE RIGHT WAY IS EVEN MORE OF A CHALLENGE

THE ULTIMATE COMPETITIVE ADVANTAGE

Truly great leaders tend to be the most simple people at heart. They are the most considerate, the most humble and the most giving. They are generous, devoted and caring. There courtesy wins the goodwill of their colleagues. They always pass on the credit to others. The importance of passion and compassion about what good leadership is and isn't has never been greater. Each day leaders should think about who they are, why they are there, and what is possible. Our world and our organizations are full of moral, ethical and civil challenges. In too many instances these attributes are sacrificed to achieve some other end. These attributes should not be sacrificed. These attributes will be the framework from which future leaders stand firm.

The better leaders will influence their organizations without knowing it. They often influence decisions without a word, but by historical expression, a gesture, or a helping hand. This is leadership.

The leader's timing is quite important. Is it time to act boldly or not? Is the organization ready, or not? What variables involving timing can be controlled. Are there variables that cannot be controlled. Is now the time???? When is the time???

Some leaders are ahead of their time. They may fight every step of the way. In some cases the organization may not be ready now, but will be ready later. Sometimes the current vision of the CEO is not implemented for one or more administrations. In some cases arrogance and being obnoxious may be appropriate in the organization for the short term. It may be that the leadership was ahead of its time with the organization. Some leaders are not actually appreciated or understood until they are gone.

Leading organizations takes time. It some cases it may take more time than you would like to succeed. Patience is hard. Leaders with a good vision can get bashed or bad-mouthed regularly. Sometimes the beatings are justifiable and sometimes they are not. The challenge is to hang on while people inside and around the organization adjust either proactively or reluctantly to change. Tough skin, a tender heart and selflessness are prerequisites to boldly moving forward.

Leadership is the ultimate competitive advantage.

-------The better leaders talk the talk, then walk the walk, then talk the talk again!

------- As a leader, does your participation make your organization better? How?

-------"You can't make the other fellow feel important in your presence if you secretly feel he is a nobody." (Les Giblin, former national salesman of the year and popular speaker)

-------"If you could win a man to your cause, you must first convince him that you are his sincere friend." (Abraham Lincoln)

-------"One of the hardest things in life is to be just as enthusiastic about the success of others as you are about your own."[46]

---

[46] Ibid-1, p. 35

-------"Some singers want the audience to love them, I love the audience." (Luciano Pavarotti, opera singer)

-------"The more you lose yourself into something bigger than yourself, the more energy you will have." (Norman Vincent Peale, pastor and author)

-------"People take action for their own reasons, not yours."

-------"The first 99.9% of achieving a goal is the determination to do it, and not to compromise no matter what sort of roadblocks come before you. The last 99.9% is working like the devil to keep you spirits up through the inevitable storms, learn something every day and serve the people around you." (S. Honda)

Life + Work + Education = Hope

Notes

1. Gilbert, Robert. (1997). More of the Best of Bits and Pieces. The Economic[i] Press. Fairfield, NJ. p176.*

2. Ibid-1, p.114.

3. Ibid-1, p.176

4. Fortune Magazine, January 1, 2015. p.86.

5. Ibid-1, p.46

6. Fortune Magazine, July 25, 2011, p. 52.

7. Gilbert, Robert. (2000). Even More of the Best of Bits and Pieces. The Economic Press. Fairfield, NJ. p. 80**

8. Ibid-1, p.8.

9. Ibid-1, p.47.

10. Ibid-1,p.252.

11. Ibid-1, p.100.

12. Ibid-1, p.191.

13. Ibid-1, p.254.

14. Ibid-1, p.107

15. Ibid-2, p.56.

16. Ibid-2, p.56.

17. Ibid-1, p.57

18. Ibid-1, p.225.

19. Ibid-1, p.227.

20. Ibid-1, p.3.

21. Ibid-1, p. 223

22. Ibid-1, p. 47

23. Ibid-1, p. 53

24. "The Word for You Today." (2016) Enon Baptist Church. December, January, February. Chester, VA. p. 45.

25. "The Word for You Today." (2012) Good Shepherd Baptist Church. June, July, August. Petersburg, VA. p.35.

26. Ibid-1, p. 45.

27. The Word, (2016).

28. The Word, (2016).

29. Ibid-2, p.37.

30. Ibid-1, p. 57,58.

31. Ibid-2, p.161.

32. Ibid-2, p. 179

33. Ibid-1, p. 157,158

34. Buettner, Dan. (2012) The Blue Zones. National Geographic Press. Washington DC. p.145.

35. Ibid-2, p.137.

36. Ibid-1, p.187.

37. Ibid-2, p.7.

38. Ibid—2, p.7

39. "The Word for You Today." (2012) Good Shepherd Baptist Church. June, July-August, Petersburg,VA. .35.

40. Ibid-1, p.42.

41. Ibid-2, p.232.

42. "The Word for You Today." (2016) Enon Baptist Church. December, January, February. Chester, VA. p.46.

43. "The Word for You Today." (2016) Enon Baptist Church. December, January, February. Chester, VA. p.45.

44. Ibid-1, p.67-68.

45. Ibid-2, p. 7

46. Ibid-1, p. 35

---

*Gilbert, Robert. (1997) More of the Best of Bits and Pieces…….. = Ibid-1.

**Gilbert, Robert. (2000) Even More of the Best of Bits and Pieces... = Ibid-2.

Pictures, Cartoons and Illustrations

Printed and bound by PG in the USA